MW01615815

A Communications Guide
for More Effective Preaching

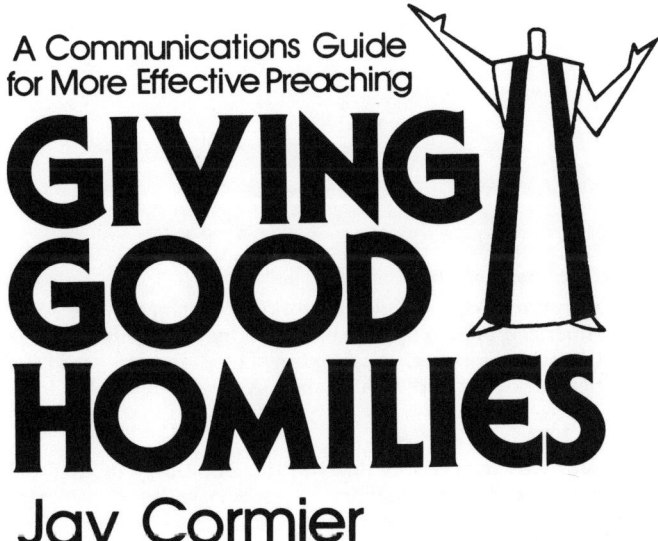

GIVING
GOOD
HOMILIES

Jay Cormier

AVE MARIA PRESS NOTRE DAME, INDIANA

For Ann

Acknowledgments:

Scripture texts used in this work are taken from the *New American Bible*, copyright © 1970 by the Confraternity of Christian Doctrine, Washington, D.C., and are used by permission of the copyright owner. All rights reserved.

Library of Congress Catalog Card Number: 84-70383

International Standard Book Number: 0-87793-317-0

Manufactured in the United States of America.

Contents

Introduction

The kingdom of heaven is like
   a man who sowed good seed in his
      field . . .
   a mustard seed . . .
   the yeast a woman used to make
      bread . . .
   a treasure hidden in the field . . .
   a dragnet cast into the sea . . .
   a king who decided to settle accounts . . .
   the owner of a vineyard . . .
   ten bridesmaids who took their lamps
      and went to meet the bridegroom . . .
   a man who entrusted property to his
      servants . . .
   a fig tree . . .

Not only is the gospel of Jesus the theological basis of good preaching, but it can give homilists invaluable insights into the technique of good preaching.

Jesus, the Word of God incarnate, spoke to the people gathered on the banks of the Sea of

Galilee and in temple precincts in words they could all understand. He spoke to them, not in the words of the Pharisees or the language of the rabbis, but with images and pictures they knew and could see in their minds. The most profound dimensions of his teachings were made clear to the shepherd, the peasant woman, and the child alike, through stories about wayward children, unscrupulous servants, poor beggars, coins and seeds. Jesus, God's perfect communication, knew how to communicate effectively with his people.

Homiletics as a *communications* skill is the theme of this book.

When I came to the Archdiocese of Washington as director of communications, the director of the Permanent Diaconate Program asked me to help assemble a series of workshops in homiletics for the deacon-candidates. One of the problems we immediately encountered was finding a good textbook for the deacons. We considered several basic college texts, including books I had used in courses and workshops I had given in the past. But the approaches in these texts were too broad for the special liturgical settings in which our deacons would be speaking—not to mention the fact that handing a 400-page tome of rhetoric and oratory (including chapters and diagrams on breath control, pitch, interpersonal communications and techniques of persuasion) might be just a little intimidating to a first-year diaconate class.

We also looked at a number of books specifically written for homiletics courses. For the most part, these books focussed on the role of the homilist as preacher and on using scripture as the basis for good preaching, rather than on the preparation and delivery of a good homily.

In reviewing the successes and failures of that first year, I began to wonder how many other homily instructors had the same problem. Several priest-friends shared with me their experience in homiletics classes in the seminary: The surprisingly vast majority of them received very little or no instruction in the communication skills of preaching—how to write for the ear, how to make a point effectively and succinctly, how to prepare one's delivery, how to emphasize thoughts and phrases through voice inflection. As my friends recalled, seminarians prepared and gave homilies in class and were critiqued by the professor, often a member of the faculty who had a "free" period.

It also struck me that, not only priests and deacons, but many more Catholics in leadership roles—Cursillo rectors, youth leaders, parish council members, religious educators, retreat team members—are speaking and making presentations before groups although they have had little or no training in speech communications.

The result of those first deacon workshops is this book. There are striking differences between this book and most other books on homiletics. First, the author is neither a priest nor a theological scholar. My background is communications, which leads to the second—the focus of this text. An understanding and appreciation of both scripture and the ministry of preaching are presumed. Therefore we will focus on homiletics as a communications process. Basic principles of communications theory—from the audience's "60-second attention span" to the "nonverbals" of public speaking—will be applied to the planning, writing and delivery of a homily.

Even though the Sunday homily is the main focus of the book, it is my hope that anyone involved in public speaking in a liturgical or church setting might find these pages helpful. For this reason, the words *homilist* and *speaker*, and *congregation* and *audience* are used interchangeably throughout the text.

There are many people who contributed to the making of this book. At the risk of omitting some, I would like to acknowledge the invaluable contributions of a few. My thanks, first, to Rev. Thomas Wells and Rev. Mr. Thomas Knestout of the Permanent Diaconate Program of the Archdiocese of Washington, who gave me the enjoyable and fulfilling challenge to work with our deacon candidates. I will always be grateful to the deacon candidates, as well, who gave me far more than I might have given them.

Thanks, too, to three good friends who reviewed the text and made invaluable contributions which made what you are about to read much better than it was the first time through the typewriter: Mr. Paul Dowd, director of Public Relations at St. Anselm College in Manchester, New Hampshire, once and always, my wise teacher and good friend; Rev. Robert Biron, a priest of the Diocese of Manchester and superb communicator in his roles as priest, homilist, teacher and friend; and Rev. W. Ronald Jameson, director of the Office of Worship of the Archdiocese of Washington whose sensitive and knowledgeable approach to the celebration of liturgy contributed to the fine tuning of many of the ideas in this book.

To Mr. Frank Cunningham and his associates at Ave Maria Press, my congratulations at having the good sense to publish this book, and my thanks for their equally good advice and counsel to this enthusiastic but sometimes verbose writer.

A special word of gratitude to three friends who graciously consented to share their homilies that follow each chapter: Revs. Robert Biron, Raymond East and Jonathan DeFelice, O.S.B.

And finally, thanks to my dearest friend, my wife Ann. Thank you for reviewing the text when it was a scattered mass of papers, for making the suggestions that had to be made when the author did not really want to listen, and for encouraging and supporting me with, "Yes, you can *too* write this book!"

I hope this book is a help to you in your ministry as a proclaimer of the Word of God. If it does offer you some assistance, please offer a prayer of thanks for the people listed above. I do.

— Jay Cormier

Chapter 1:

The Thought Work of a Homily

Father B. was studying for an advanced degree in scripture so he could return to his diocese and teach in the seminary. During the semester, he helped out at a suburban parish in the Washington, D.C., area. The parish was made up of mostly low-to-moderate-income families; more than half were minorities living in several housing projects in the vicinity.

On his first Sunday in the parish, after the deacon finished the proclamation of the gospel, Father B. went to the lectern and began his homily.

"My dear friends. In even the most cursory exegesis of this morning's gospel. . . ."

Exegesis? What's an exegesis? It's a safe bet that 99 percent of the people sitting in that church had no idea what Father B. was talking about. Sadder still, when Father B. completed his 20-minute journey through Scripture Seminar

101, nobody in the church really cared to know what this ex-a-whatever was all about.

The word was soon out. If at all possible, avoid the Masses during which "that theologian guy with all the big words" was going to preach.

This particular incident (which actually occurred) could be charitably termed a failure in communications. Why? The reasons started long before Father B. stepped up to the lectern that Sunday morning.

Any exchange of messages—from writing a school textbook to airing a Miller Lite commercial—begins with what advertising people call *audience analysis.* Whom do we want to reach? What do we want to tell them? How do we want them to react or respond to this message?

Not a word is written, not a photograph is taken, not a scene is filmed until those questions have been completely answered.

Let's run through the basic questions of a pre-homily audience analysis. Now, these questions might seem to be very elementary and simplistic. Yet most of the time a homily or talk doesn't work because the speakers do not understand the audience they are addressing.

For any talk, the first thing that has to be done is to select the *subject.* Sometimes, the speaker is given a subject to talk about;

sometimes the speaker picks the subject. More often than not, however, the subject at the start is very broad—so large, in fact, that it is unmanageable. The real work in selecting the subject is often selecting one of the many topics possible within that one, vast, original subject.

When I was a diocesan communications director in New England, I was invited by an area Lions' Club to be the guest speaker at one of its luncheon meetings. The program chairman asked me to talk about "The Catholic Church in Our Community." I had 20 minutes, right after lunch.

"Hmmm," I said to myself, "what meaningful, insightful things can I say to give these gentlemen a complete and total picture of all the many ministries of the church in our community—in 20 minutes?" As you can see, this is very much like being asked: "Explain the political, military and economic dimensions of the Hundred Years' War—in 25 words or less."

So the process for putting that talk together began by my asking myself: What do I really know about the Catholic Church that would interest this group of middle-aged businessmen, particularly after a weekday luncheon when most have to get back to their offices and stores? What can I concisely but completely cover in 20 minutes?

Well, under that general topic of "The Catholic Church in Our Community" there were hundreds of topics I could have addressed. I could have talked about the Catholic school system, what the diocese projected for future enrollments and the impact of Catholic schools on local public schools; or I could have talked about the new soup kitchen that had just been opened by our social ministries department—why it was opening and what these businessmen could do to help.

But it had just been announced, after weeks of rumors, that Pope John Paul II was going to spend the first day of his 1979 visit to the United States in Boston, less than 50 miles away. With all the excitement the news of the pope's visit had generated, what better topic to address?

I ended up spending a very enjoyable 20 minutes talking about the details of the Holy Father's visit that were set, the logistics for New Hampshire residents to come to Boston to see the pope, and—perhaps most important of all, especially for a group that included many non-Catholics—why John Paul was coming and why both his visit and his office are so important to Catholics. In pointing to the themes of justice and peace that the pope said he was going to address during his U.S. visit, it was quite easy and natural to point out that every ministry of the church flows from the church's commitment to Christ's gospel command "to love one another as I have loved you." The same commitment to justice and peace that was bringing the pope to the U.S. leads New Hampshire Catholics to build schools and open soup kitchens for the poor ". . . *in Our Community.*"

Selecting a subject for any speech involves five basic considerations:

1. *Choosing a subject that you, the speaker, know about and are familiar with.* If you were an English major in college, chances are you are never going to be able to give an inspiring, rousing discourse on "The Joys of Calculus."

In much the same way, it is very difficult for a homilist who has no contact with older adults in the parish to communicate any real understanding of the plight of the aged. He might be able to rattle off the standard cliches about loneliness and the difficulty of living on a fixed income, but it is very hard to imagine a homilist who has no personal experience with the aged inspiring the rest of the parish to come to the aid of their older neighbors.

2. *Choosing something that interests you.* No matter how much you read and study, you are never going to give an interesting or meaningful talk on ballet if you dislike ballet.

Homilists sometimes find themselves talking about something that really doesn't interest them in the slightest. In my parish, I can always tell which are the really important second collections and which ones the pastor doesn't care much about.

3. *Choosing something that interests your audience.* This is the other side of the coin. To use a previous example, you may love ballet and you may think that Baryshnikov is the greatest dancer on the stage, but no presentation on Baryshnikov is going to work in an address before the members of the Washington Redskins Gridiron Club. Now some Gridiron members might be interested in ballet, but certainly not the whole group. Remember that this group has convened for one reason: the Redskins. Now if you can somehow bridge the ideas of ballet and football (and it can be done!), you have something.

Again, this might seem too elementary and logical to even discuss here. Of course a speaker has to interest the audience; but that was a major problem of Father B.'s homily. *Exegesis* is a scripture scholar's word—not an insurance salesman's word, nor a housewife's word, nor a truck driver's word, nor a teacher's word, nor a student's word. As his homily developed, Father B. said nothing that meant anything to the people gathered for that liturgy.

4. *Choosing a subject that is neither above nor below the comprehension of your audience.* Discussing Little League baseball with the management of the Yankees, or explaining the impact of cable television revenues on major league player-owner arbitration to the Elm Street Astros of the South Park Little League are about the same in terms of bad timing and poor communications.

This is a real problem in any preaching. Because the congregation is often made up of people of different ages, backgrounds and professions, finding a topic of interest to such a diverse community can often be a problem. There is real wisdom in designating Masses for children, folk liturgies for younger parishioners, and more traditional approaches to liturgy for older members of the parish community.

Father B.'s experience illustrates a common problem homilists can have in speaking above the congregation's level of understanding. Many homilists use words, concepts and phrases that mean nothing to the folks sitting there. It is a common problem for any presenter who speaks in jargon. Be careful of using theological jargon—the same words used in the latest theological journals are not the same words used by the people of the parish.

5. *Choosing a subject that can be adequately and responsibly covered in the time available.* Many a homiletics class has heard the legends of the great Saint Augustine and how people would travel for miles to hear the holy bishop preach for up to 10 hours at a time! That is, indeed, quite a feat! God must surely have inspired Augustine in a special way.

One question: What else did those poor people have to do on a Sunday? Gutenberg and his magic printing machine were still about a millennium away, with radio and television just under two millennia into the future. Illiteracy was the rule rather than the exception. The performing arts were little more than poetic rituals witnessed by relatively few people. To hear a great orator like Augustine preach in his cathedral then was as exciting as having orchestra seats for the biggest musical on Broadway in our time.

What today's preachers—indeed, anyone who speaks before any group—have to contend with is the 60-second attention span. We are bombarded every day with thousands and thousands of messages. Television especially has conditioned us to absorb information in 30- and 60-second audiovisual clips. Sorry, but Saint Augustine's act just would not fly in today's information age.

Quite often people lament: Oh, if the church could only come up with another great television preacher like Bishop Fulton J. Sheen! There is no question that Bishop Sheen was one of the great preachers of our time. But could a Bishop Sheen-style speaker attract large audiences on television today? Probably not.

The technology of television has developed light-years beyond what it was 30 years ago. Television's new electronics not only affect how a program is presented but what is presented as well. Even though viewers don't know the technical why's and wherefore's of computerized graphics, instant satellite transmissions, microwave remote cameras, and the like, they do expect to see the effects of this television wizardry when they tune in their favorite programs. Vintage Fulton Sheen and his chalkboard would have a very difficult time making the impact in today's wide world of television that he made in the 1950s.

That doesn't mean that the art of rhetoric is lost forever; it does mean that if you want to communicate faith from the pulpit, you have to realize at the start that in the mass media-oriented society of which your parishioners are a part, your typical listener's attention span is quite short. People simply will not sit and listen for very long periods of time.

I have heard very few speakers who are naturally fascinating, funny and/or entertaining enough to keep a congregation enthralled for more than a few minutes.

So *time*—not how much time the program allows you, but how much time the audience/congregation gives you—is a major consideration in planning a homily.

Once the subject is determined, narrowed in scope and defined, the second question to answer in the homily thought process is: What is the *purpose* of this talk or homily? Why am I giving this talk? What do I want to accomplish with this presentation?

If your response is: "Well, the rubrics say I've got to say something after the gospel," your problem is not one of speech communications, but a basic vocation-ministry crisis.

But if you enjoy your ministry and if you deeply care about your people, then the question of purpose calls for more profound consideration. Why preach this homily? More specifically, what effect should these words have on the listeners?

Do you want to inform them of something? Do you want them to feel something? Do you simply want them to feel good about themselves?

Now all of this may seem too simple even to mention. Certainly the subject and the purpose of any talk has to be determined at the outset, but the point is to keep that subject and purpose in the forefront as you put together the homily. Too often speakers lose sight of their purpose and begin to ramble on and on about things that have little to do with either the topic or the listeners, resulting in the audience wondering what that was all about.

The third factor to consider in this pre-homily analysis is *the audience.* The potential listeners should have a very definite effect on what words will be used to communicate the intended message.

So before stepping up to the lectern to dazzle the people of God, think about the following:

First, the size of the audience. If the Mass is to be celebrated with a small group of people, the homilist has to avoid being formal to the point of being stiff or remote. The old chestnut about the minister who comes into church to find only one of the town's farmers in the congregation contains a great deal of wisdom. The minister decides that he's going to give the same sermon he had planned, regardless of the number in the church. So, for the next hour, the minister pours it on, all for the benefit of this one farmer sitting in this big empty church. After the service, the minister meets the farmer in the front of the church and asks him what he thought of the sermon. "Oh, it was real good," the farmer replied, "but if I called all my chickens to supper and only one came, I don't think I'd feed it the whole bag of grain."

The converse is true as well. In front of a large Sunday congregation, the homilist can't very well sit down at the edge of the sanctuary and chat with the congregation. In a formal church setting, people expect the homilist to speak from the place designated for that purpose (the lectern) and with some formality (which does not mean being stiff, pompous or trite). Some of the Sunday communicants may like the "rapping with the folks" approach, but probably most will care little or dislike it altogether, and consequently will not hear the message being communicated in the homily.

The environment can have a positive or negative effect on a speech. The homilist should consider if the place for this liturgy is conducive to prayer. Will the people be physically comfortable during the homily or speech? Those metal folding chairs common to every church in the country have done more to destroy the art of preaching than some of the world's worst preachers.

What about the place from which the homilist will speak: Can he be clearly seen from every place in the congregation? Is there proper lighting in the sanctuary so the congregation can see the homilist and the homilist can see his or her notes?

Is a public address system required? If so, can one be obtained and installed that works properly, without feedback and reverberation? After those cursed folding chairs, inadequate public address systems have resulted in a large number of homiletic catastrophes. It is amazing the number of parishes that have built physically beautiful churches and work hard to maintain them, and yet have installed public address systems carelessly and thoughtlessly, making the congregations feel that they are in a minor-league baseball park rather than in the house of God.

A director friend of mine always says: "You can't do Shakespeare in Grand Central Station." Some sanctuaries are ideally planned for big liturgies with crowds of people, but in that same space, a smaller, more intimate liturgy is lost. Some smaller churches are little more than concrete boxes, designed to be used for so many purposes that they really fail to fulfill any function very well.

Whatever the environment, homilists should be aware of what effect that space is going to have on their presentations and their reception by the audience, and what might be done ahead of time to correct any problems.

Age is a factor in a pre-homily audience study. Obviously, a homilist can't talk about transubstantiation with the second-grade First Communion class; and the priest or deacon is not going to get very far with the Golden Agers if he illustrates a point with rock music from the latest pop music survey.

The values of the audience/congregation should also be realized and understood by the homilist/speaker. It is very difficult to understand and deal with a set of values that may be the antithesis of what the homilist believes. In Bill C. Davis' wonderful Broadway play, *Mass Appeal,* the young deacon, Mark, is having a great deal of trouble preaching without offending his congregation with thunderous denunciations of their materialistic values and lifestyles. In discussing the problem with the pastor, Mark laments, "I don't mean to offend them. It's just that I love these people and I know what they can become!" But the wiser, more experienced pastor shoots back, "But what about what they are?!"

Exactly where are these people in relationship to the subject to be addressed in the homily? Be very careful about the answer. The question is not where you would like them to be or where you think they should be on the subject. Where are they? What do they value as important? Are you able to accept the fact that what you are going to talk about, even though it may be the very essence of the gospel, may be received with anger, suspicion, or indifference?

And make no mistake about this fact, as well: People respond only when they see something in it for themselves. There has to be some kind of reward or gratification. It may be monetary or it may be emotional, like the joy of doing something good. It may be a new insight or information that will, at some time, be beneficial to them.

This value system affects other aspects of communication as well, such as language. A priest I know gave a wonderful homily to a First Eucharist class by simply walking down the aisle from the altar, taking a hand microphone, and talking directly to the children. The priest totally ignored the adults in the church and talked directly to the group of 35 seven-year-olds, explaining in very simple language how the Eucharistic bread was a gift from Jesus, that it was a piece of himself, and what Jesus expects from us in return for the gift. Father knew whom he was talking to and what they could understand and appreciate. He reached those children and in his sincerity and simplicity I suspect he reached a few of the adults too.

Now I know another priest who takes a hand mike every Sunday and walks up and down the aisle during his homily. Some people like it, but many people in the congregation do not. The negative effect on these people far outweighs the positive impact on those who like it. I overheard one parishioner say, "Oh look, here comes Monty Hall in vestments." Many a good homily has not been communicated because of some ill-advised risk-taking like that.

The occasion also affects an audience's response. What is appropriate on one occasion may be totally out of place on another. There is a wonderful story called *Barrington Bunny,* a parable by Martin Bell about a little rabbit who freezes to death in order to keep a little field mouse warm the night of a blizzard. The story is a hopeful one, however, because Barrington comes to understand the purpose of his being a warm and furry bunny and the joy there is in sharing what we are. We've used the story as part of a Christmas radio program, and I know many religious educators who have used the story to help children understand the mystery of Easter.

But one priest used the story at a funeral Mass for an adult. To say it didn't work is putting it mildly. The reactions ranged from "Father is trivializing our loss with a bunny story" to "He must think we're kids." The point here is not that the story is bad and says nothing about life and resurrection; the point is that on that particular occasion with that particular audience the story was not appropriate.

There is still one more attitude of the audience to discern: their attitude toward the homilist—you. How do these folks feel about you preaching to them on this topic?

In one sense, this book is a perfect example of the issue. I am a layman. I've given very few homilies in the strictest sense. The few scripture courses I took in my undergraduate days hardly make me an authority in scripture. So why should priests and ministers read my book on how to preach a sermon?

Because this book is about speech communications, which is a subject I do know something about and, I guess since you've read this far, you, the reader, accept me as an authority on the subject. Should I have started this book with a long diatribe on scripture and criticized the theological content of today's sermons, readers would (and should) take this book back for a refund.

The occasion, too, makes this book more acceptable. More and more men and women are finding themselves in situations where they have to preach or address an audience: for example, those preparing for ordination to the permanent diaconate. Many of these "homilists" have no formal training at all in public speaking.

So, too, members of the congregation/audience are asking similar questions about the preacher. Nothing makes them question a homilist's credibility more quickly than even hinting at a particular stand on a political or controversial issue.

"Father ought to stick to God. What does he know about foreign policy!?"

"What does the pastor know about sex and marriage? God, he's probably never even dated!"

"Humph! Listen to *him* talk about poverty! Him with his Buick in the rectory garage. And he doesn't have to worry about where his next meal is going to come from."

And so on. . . .

Giving any kind of presentation—be it a lecture in a college classroom, a sales presentation, or a homily—means putting one's credibility on the line. An important question, therefore, at the beginning of the homily process is: Do I have the credibility to talk about this question or issue? Will the parishioners accept me as believable and credible in what I say?

This is one of the most difficult aspects of preaching, particularly for newly ordained deacons. The first time the deacon finds himself in the pulpit—*up* there instead of *down* there with the folks—it can be a frightening experience. And that's understandable.

But the situation is not totally negative. Ordination itself, first of all, is a very credible thing. Ordination creates a bond, a trust between ministers and the people they serve. Some would use the word *authority* in explaining that bond. However it is described, the fact is that ordination gives the minister a stature in the eyes of parishioners from which he should draw the courage to preach. A similar kind of *stature* also exists for the teacher in the eyes of students, or the vowed religious in the eyes of a group of retreatants.

But keep in mind that this "built-in credibility" is a very fragile thing. Years ago, when the priest was the only one in the village who had an education beyond basic reading and arithmetic, his word was law. Today, though, Father is not the only one in the church with education, training and experience. Many of his parishioners will know more than he does about many things.

But homilists offer listeners a new perspective on the world, a view of the world based on faith. The homilist is one of God's human creatures, who also struggles with the same questions that they do. But the homilist brings to the people Christ's light to illuminate life's darkest passages.

If the homilists' love and concern is sincere for the people participating in the liturgy, if their desire is sincere to share rather than impose the good news, and if they are sincere when addressing the listeners as "brothers and sisters," or "dear friends in Christ," the attitude of the audience won't be a problem.

The importance of thinking about the audience who will hear the homily-in-the-making cannot be overemphasized. Advertisers spend millions of dollars in scientific audience analysis and research. Procter and Gamble, McDonald's, and all the other giant corporations with the megabuck advertising budgets spend a great deal of time and money finding out who is going to be watching their commercials at a given *time*, and what *images*, *ideas*, and *concepts* will be most appealing to them and predispose them to buy the product. After all of this information is determined and understood, then the commercials are made and the television time is bought.

Granted, you're not selling soap or hamburgers. You're sharing faith. Doesn't that deserve the same kind of effort?

A Homily

Homily for the 15th Sunday in Ordinary Time (B)

Reading 1, Am 7:12-15: Go, prophesy to my people.

Responsorial, Ps 85: Lord, let us see your kindness.

Reading 2, Eph 1:3-14: Before the world was made, he chose us in Christ.

Gospel, Mk 6:7-13: He called the Twelve, and began to send them out.

(1)   Remember the last time you packed for a trip? There are so many things to think of! What's the weather going to be like? Will I need my heavy jacket? Should I take my umbrella? What shoes should I bring with which suit or dress?

(2)   If you're like me, you don't want to leave without *everything* you'll really need. And then, when you're finally packed up and ready to go, you drive yourself crazy with those nagging questions: Do I have my ticket? Did I pack my medicine? What about my extra pair of glasses?

(3)   Now, try and imagine how much more difficult your packing would be if you had no idea *where* you were going or *how long* you'd be gone!

(4) In this morning's gospel, Jesus sent his disciples on just such a mysterious journey (Mk 6:7-13). Imagine their surprise when the master tells them to leave their "Palestine Tourister" luggage behind—in fact, they're to take with them hardly anything at all!

(5) And just what was this urgent "Mission of the Twelve" all about? It was related to the prophet Amos' mission to the people of Israel (Am 7:12-15). "Off with you, visionary!" God told Amos. "Prophesy!" And the message to be proclaimed is beautifully summarized in Psalm 85 that we read together a moment ago: "Near indeed is his salvation to those who fear him."

(6) St. Paul, in his letter to the Ephesians (Eph 1:3-14), sees Jesus' mission that he sends the Twelve—and you and me—as having three steps:

First, God chose *us*—you and me—before the world began. He chose us to be holy, God-like and filled "to the brim" with his love;

Second, in Christ and through his blood we've been redeemed, forgiven, saved—so boundless is God's love for us; and

Third, the plan is that in Christ *we*—again, you and I—will bring all things into one under Christ's headship.

(7) So it's quite a journey we are all on. Every one of us has been sent forth! Your hospital bed or your sickbed at home can be

the vehicle for this journey if you let Jesus
send you forth. You don't need to carry
anything. Who can tell what new friends you
may encounter, what new lives you may
touch! Your patient witness to the sufferings of
Christ is a testimony that speaks more elo-
quently than any words can.

(8)　　I've spoken with nurses and medical
personnel and family members whose lives
have been deeply touched by the witness to
God given by elderly and infirm loved ones
and patients.

(9)　　Is it easy to proclaim the kingdom of
God? No. Might your message be rejected?
Quite possibly. Such was the case of the
Twelve. But Jesus promises us his help and his
grace. If we embark on the journey, then the
Lord will supply us with everything we need to
carry out *our* mission.

Comments

The celebrant preached this homily during the Sunday Mass televised each week on a Washington, D.C., station. Father had two major considerations to keep in mind as he planned his homily: The vast majority of his congregation would be older and others ill and bedridden; and he would have only a half-hour for the entire Mass (which is really 28 minutes and 30 seconds in television time), so he would have no more than four minutes for the homily. Almost anyone can preach for 10 or 20 minutes; it takes real communication skill to say something meaningful in only two or three minutes.

The opening paragraphs of this homily immediately set up a good relationship between the homilist and his audience. All of us have packed for a trip, and most of us do second-guess our packing decisions and wonder, "Do I have everything?" The reference to medicine and glasses is particularly meaningful to the television audience—whenever my grandmother went anywhere, the first things she put in her bag were her pills and an extra pair of glasses.

From that introduction, the homilist then asks the congregation to consider the human dimensions of the gospel story (paragraphs three and four). Father asks that we consider the consequences and ramifications of what Jesus is asking of the Twelve (and of us) in embarking on this journey. This mission demands an attitude not limited by material resources of food, clothing and money.

From the examples cited in paragraphs seven and eight, it is clear Father knows his audience. He effectively relates the theme of the three readings to the day-to-day life situations of the viewers. The homilist has given careful consideration to the three major questions discussed in the preceding chapter:

— *Defining the subject:* determining the theme of the lectionary readings.

— *Determining the purpose of the homily:* to offer encouragement, to make the congregation feel that they, too, are part of the church and the church's mission.

— *Analyzing the audience:* who they are, their needs, their attitudes and beliefs.

To become an effective homilist, be "tuned in" to the people who will be "tuning in" to you.

Chapter 2:

Homily Under Construction

"The kingdom of heaven is like . . . ."
—*The Gospel of St. Matthew*

In his gospel account, Matthew goes to great lengths to point out that Jesus "taught the crowds in the form of parables. He spoke to them in parables only to fulfill what had been said through the prophet:

'I will open my mouth in parables,
I will announce what has lain hidden
  since the creation of the world' "
(Mt 13:34-35)

Parables . . . stories . . . images from life's everyday experiences . . . pictures and events that people can see, feel and understand. From mustard seeds, fishing nets and errant sons, Jesus enabled his listeners to grasp the meaning of the deepest mysteries of faith: God the Creator as Father of all humanity, the dawning of the new kingdom of God, the joys of simple charity.

The most effective homilies are really a form of storytelling—not long narratives with intricate plots and a full cast of characters, but real images that people know and see and feel. Sometimes a homily's story will have all of the dramatic elements of plot, climax and resolution; often, however, the kind of story meant here will tell itself in the imaginations of your listeners. Using the right image or idea will trigger the listener's own story—personal experiences based on encountering the image. From those stories a homilist can share faith that is meaningful and real.

So, with this concept of storytelling in mind, let's take a look at the process of writing the homily. Remember that thus far we have done the thought work—defining and focusing on one subject, deciding the purpose of the homily, and coming to a clear understanding of the audience/congregation who will hear this presentation.

The first step in writing a talk or homily is what professional communicators understand as *research*—the gathering of facts, details and data to support the points the speaker wishes to make or to aid the speaker in determining the points that should be made on the chosen topic. In preparing a homily, we are not talking about burying one's self in the library with textbooks, volumes of reference works and computer print-outs. Research for the homilist means spending time with the lectionary readings for the Mass.

A friend of mine, who is an excellent homilist, always reads the scripture selections for the following Sunday on the previous Sunday night, just before going to bed, and then reads them again every morning that week. He also consults scripture commentaries early in the week to get a clear idea of the context of the reading. Throughout the week he works over the ideas of those three readings in his mind. Usually some personal experience—something he reads, something somebody says to him, something that happens around the rectory—triggers a story that crystalizes the theme of those readings.

When reading the scripture selections for the Mass, consider two questions.

What is the common theme of these three readings? Where do the Old and New Testament readings selected for this particular Sunday intersect to tell us something about our own experience as Christians in this century?

A second question to reflect upon: What are the human dimensions of these readings that strike the reader/hearer? Think about how and why the characters say and act as they do. Consider, too, the historical context of these readings. Parables that have become tired tales can often take on fresh, new meanings; mysteriously vague prophecies can become clear and relevant to today's world.

Consider the following two examples from the gospels.

Everyone has heard the story of the Good Samaritan. The message is clear: Christian love demands that we care about all of our neighbors. But keep in mind the historical context of the story. In Jesus' time, the Jews considered the Samaritans outcasts and heretics—Samaritans and Jews were not invited to the same party. So, Christ made a great deal of impact by portraying a Samaritan as the hero in his parable.

We all admire the Good Samaritan for his compassion, but do we really give him enough credit? By our standards, the Samaritan would be looked upon with a great deal of suspicion. When he saw the poor man lying in the road after being beaten and robbed, the Good Samaritan didn't stop to consider who the man was or what his own people would think if he helped this poor Jew, nor did the Samaritan consider what helping the Jew would cost in terms of time and money. How often do we let labels complicate what would otherwise be a clear sense of duty to respond in charity? How many ways can we find to rationalize a decision not to respond to someone in need? Perhaps there's more to the Good Samaritan story than we might first think.

In St. John's Gospel, Jesus asks Peter three times if he loves him. After Peter responds each time that he does, indeed, love the Lord, Jesus commissions Peter "to feed my lambs, feed my sheep." This Easter reading recalls Christ's establishing his church on Peter the "Rock," the first pope, and its mission in the world.

But think about the human side of this story for a moment. Not once, not twice, but three times Jesus questions Peter's love for him. As we read the incident (Jn 21:15-19), we can feel Peter's bewilderment and hurt that Jesus, whom Peter has followed for the past three years, simply won't take his word that he loves Jesus. Remembering how he and the other apostles scattered after Jesus' arrest and crucifixion, Peter probably felt like a traitor and coward, as well, and was painfully aware why Jesus would question his love.

Now suppose the person or persons you love most in this world—your spouse, your child, your parents—continually questioned your love for them. Now we can understand how Peter feels. We can feel his pain and understand how desperately he must have wanted to prove his love for Jesus once and for all. At first reading this incident is the birth of the papacy, but when we look at the human side of this exchange between Jesus and Peter, the incident becomes a powerful story of commitment and love.

Like any presentation, the writing of a homily begins with research—not a data search but a spiritual search. What is God saying to us in the Sunday readings? How does the historical context affect the theme of a particular passage in relation to the other assigned readings? Regarding the characters in these scripture readings, what are the human dimensions—emotions, difficulties, doubts—that we can relate to from our own experience?

A homilist's research of the lectionary readings should result in some ideas to share with the congregation on Sunday. Now the homilist should start writing, making a list of the things to say in the homily—whatever strikes the homilist about the readings: some historical fact found in a commentary, some event or experience that parallels the theme of the readings. This list of ideas is the second step in the speech-writing process.

The third step is to take those points and put them into some kind of logical order or systematic sequence. Basically, three kinds of sequences facilitate an audience's grasp of the ideas a speaker wants to communicate:

Chronological sequence: presenting ideas in the order in which they happen. In any presentation on World War II in the Pacific, the bombing of Pearl Harbor should be mentioned before the signing of the armistice on the *U.S.S. Missouri.* In explaining how to make an omelette, the speaker should mention the cracking of eggs before the garnishing with clove. This chapter—in fact, this whole book—is an example of chronological sequence. Chances are, unless the homilist is explaining the events that have led up to a parish program or explaining how to do something, he or she will not use this system in putting a homily together.

From the familiar to the unfamiliar: starting with the things that the average person in the pew knows, and then proceeding to the things he or she may not know.

From the concrete to the abstract: starting with a representation that the audience can see, hear or feel to enable them to understand and appreciate an idea or concept.

All of Jesus' parables work in either of these two latter systems. For example, Jesus explains the different effects of the word of God on different people by using the example of the sower. Everyone listening understood how seeds are planted and how different soil conditions affect their growth (the familiar). Through the example of the sower, Jesus' audience could understand his point: how and why people hear and respond to God's word differently (the unfamiliar).

The crowds that heard the Sermon on the Mount were all familiar with what salt did for their food and with the importance of oil lamps at night in their homes (the concrete). When Jesus called on them to be "salt for the earth" and "light before men so that they may see goodness in your acts" (the abstract), they understood exactly what the Lord was asking of them.

At this point in the writing process, the homilist should have a good idea of the message he or she wants to communicate. We now come to the most important part of the homily—the *introduction*. It's a fact of liturgical life: If you don't capture the congregation's attention in the first 15 to 30 seconds, you might as well go right into the Creed and collection. We've all listened—or stopped listening—to speakers who just failed to interest us at the very beginning of their presentation and we simply turned them off. What they had to say might have been very important and of great benefit to us, but those first words, those first utterances we heard from the speaker's mouth, had the effect of "forget this; this is going to be a waste of my time."

And then we have all heard the speaker who said just the right things that captured our attention and imagination immediately, making us want to hear what was to come. That speaker somehow established rapport with us, identified with our interests, signalled to us that what was going to be said would inform us, benefit us or entertain us.

But the introduction is more than just a snappy attention-grabber. It is the story discussed earlier. It is the homilist's parable—the image, event or experience through which the speaker communicates a dimension of faith.

In a well-thought-out and well-constructed homily, the entire message flows naturally from the story shared at the beginning. The image or idea presented in the opening should trigger within the listeners' imaginations their own stories and experiences. Through those stories, faith can be communicated and shared.

Several devices can be used in the beginning of a speech/homily to effectively tell the story you want to share.

One such device is a simple *reference to the subject or the occasion.* Some occasions and topics are so important to the audience that speakers can establish almost instant rapport by telling them at the outset that they, too, share

this concern, or in the joy or sorrow of the occasion. During those first tense weeks of the court-
ordered busing of schoolchildren in Boston a few
years ago, one homilist began a Sunday sermon:
"It's been a tough, frightening week for all of us,
whether we're a student, a parent, a teacher or
educator, or a resident." Establishing that em-
pathy with the congregation at the very beginning was the most direct and effective way of
getting listeners' attention. The best homilies I
have heard at weddings have begun simply by
the celebrant saying, "Bob and Donna, thank
you for letting us be part of this very important
day in your lives. . . ."

A *personal reference or experience* is another
effective way of starting a homily. The homilist,
too, is wrestling with what God is saying in these
scripture readings, just as the listeners are. Good,
caring homilists want to share their humanness
with the others who have gathered around the
altar.

On an Ash Wednesday, Father began his
homily with this reminiscence: "When I was a
kid, I had to take piano lessons. I'll always
remember what my teacher said to me one day. I
didn't appreciate what he was saying to me then,
but as I get older, I understand more and more.
He said to me, 'Thomas, anyone can play the
notes on this page of music. The beauty comes in

the pause between the notes.' " From that point, Father developed the idea of the Lenten season being a time for a "pause between the notes" of our lives, and inviting participation in the parish's Lenten services and programs.

Politicians have mastered the use of the *rhetorical question* in beginning a speech: "Are your taxes too high?" "Do you want to leave your children an environment that will shorten their lives by as much as 50 years?" "Do you think the time has come for America to stop getting pushed around by second- and third-rate powers?" And so it goes.

In some homily situations, a well-phrased rhetorical question might get the faith community thinking about God's word in ways they might not have before. Jesus quite effectively used the rhetorical question in demonstrating his Father's relationship with us: "Which one among you would give your child a snake when he asks for bread?"

Quotations can be another effective device in beginning a homily—but not a quotation from scripture. When a celebrant begins his homily with a quote from the Sunday gospel and then solemnly intones the sign of the cross—that's a sure turn-off for many of us. It says, first of all, that Father is going to follow a sermon format that is associated with a lot of terrible sermons, that the chances are slim that we're going to hear anything new or different or applicable to our lives, that Father thinks we're dumb and won't remember the text of the gospel.

Am I being unfair? Yes, I am. Does that mean you can't give a good sermon by starting out with the biblical text? No, it doesn't. The fact of the matter is that I, the person you are trying to communicate with, am turned off to that kind of introduction, having been conditioned by many, many bad sermons that started off exactly that way. I may not be fair, but I am being honest. If homilists feel compelled to repeat the text at the very beginning of the sermon (the "sledgehammer approach" in homiletics), they are only displaying a lack of confidence, either in their own ability to make the desired point, or in the congregation's ability to understand it.

The quotation device is most effective when the quotation is not biblical. Famous poems, lines from plays, even a commercial slogan, can help people understand and focus on an idea from their perspective. The fact is, more people are reading Robert Ludlum than Karl Barth, or visiting the Golden Arches than the theology section of the Catholic book store.

Everyone in the late 1960s knew the big line from the Eric Segal movie, *Love Story:* "Love means never having to say you're sorry." Well,

one homilist I remember used that line to launch
a beautiful homily on forgiveness (the fact that I
remember it almost 20 years later says something
for it). "Maybe Eric Segal has it wrong," he
began, "maybe love means *being able* to say
you're sorry. . . ."

There are so many examples of books,
plays, poems and television shows, from
Shakespeare to M*A*S*H, that speak the values
of the gospel. Often it is just a matter of making
the connection.

Sometimes startling an audience with a fact
or an opinion can capture their attention. One
speaker told a youth group about Thomas Mer-
ton—monk, teacher, mystic, playboy and com-
munist. What? Come again? That little bombshell
at the outset set the stage for a reflection on life
as a journey, a series of decisions and changes.

In *Life* magazine, author Morris L. West
began a piece on the death of the beloved Pope
John XXIII by asking: "Will they canonize him
and make him officially a saint in the calendar?
In a way I hope not. . . ."

Good Lord, why not?

"I want to remember him for what he
was—a loving man, a simple priest, a good
pastor and a builder of bridges across which we
poor devils may hope to scramble one day for
salvation."

One of the most difficult themes to preach about, I believe, is Mary, the Mother of God. I received that insight from a sermon I heard some time ago in which the priest began his homily by saying exactly that—that he was uncomfortable, almost embarrassed, to talk about Mary. This certainly caught the attention of the assembled faithful—especially the Blue Army folks (and they were a pretty large contingent in our parish). "You see," Father continued, "I'm having trouble with this because of what we've done to her. Oh, there's nothing wrong with honoring Mary as Queen of this or Our Lady of that. But, for me, the greatest thing about Mary was her humanity, her desire to accept the difficult task God was placing before her, her heartfelt sense of charity and duty toward Elizabeth. . . ." For the first time, I (and I suspect not just a few members of the Rosary Society) saw Mary, not as a lovely ivory statue, but as a real woman.

Two other devices are probably the most effective of all in introducing a homily—and they are also the most dangerous.

One is *humor.* When a joke works, it is gangbusters. But when it bombs, the tremors can be felt for miles and hours.

Some people cannot tell a joke. It's as simple as that. It takes an extraordinary amount of confidence and timing to tell a joke to a group. Very few newly ordained priests, deacons and ministers possess that kind of confidence and facility the first few times they step up to the lectern. So try it only if you are sure of both the joke and of your ability to tell it.

If you are going to use an opening joke or humorous anecdote, make sure, first of all, that no one will be offended by the joke. If you suspect that someone—anyone—may be offended or not understand it, do not use it. As we discussed in sizing up the audience in the last chapter, the issue is not whether the joke is, in fact, good, bad, funny, or offensive, but how the audience will perceive it.

Humor does not have to sting. In one workshop for deacons, I asked the group, as one of their first assignments, to prepare a short talk in which they introduce the members of the parish staff to new parishioners. One of the deacons, in the course of his introductions, introduced the pastor with a lot of barbs. Unless you knew the pastor (and knew him well) the comments were, frankly, insulting. Some of the jokes were "inside jokes" that only a close-knit staff would understand and appreciate. We were not "in" on the jokes, and the inexperienced deacon was making no effort to explain them to us. Instead of enjoying the jokes, we were all becoming uncomfortable and embarrassed.

There's a fine line between good-natured teasing and really hurting someone. Be extremely careful not to cross that line should you decide to go that road.

Make sure the joke or anecdote fits the theme the homily is going to address. Many priests have the reputation of being regular Henny Youngmans and Milton Berles in the pulpit. They feel that they just can't give a sermon without starting off with a few jokes and one-liners. Father really has them rolling in the aisles, but he is not saying anything; no faith is being shared. After a while, Father Yuks wears a little thin.

A priest began a homily with the following story:

Father was visiting a First Communion class. During his visit, Father decided to find out how well the children were learning their catechism taught by the Sisters. He asked little Becky, "What is Easter?"

"Easter," Becky said, "is the day when our family gets together and has a big turkey dinner to thank God for everything in the world."

"No, that's not quite right, Becky." Father asked the next child the same question.

"Easter," the little boy said, "is when we all dress up like ghosts and witches and go all over the neighborhood for candy."

"Ah, no," the priest said, who was becoming a bit exasperated. Father then called on little Freddy and asked him what Easter was.

Freddy began: "Easter is when Jesus, after he was crucified, was buried in the tomb and three days later rose from the dead."

"Exactly right!" said the jubilant priest.

"And," Freddy continued, "if Jesus sees his shadow we have six more weeks of winter."

From that story, the homilist asked the congregation to consider how well we understand the mystery of Easter, whether our daily lives reflect our professed hope in Christ's victory over the grave. The joke was well told by the homilist. More importantly, it was an excellent setting for the homily's message of living and understanding the Easter mystery.

The use of *media* can be a very effective way to capture an audience's attention, but a recording, film or slide presentation is also fraught with dangers.

While media is being incorporated more and more into liturgy, some communicants still do not like movies during Mass. Be sensitive to that.

Some well-intentioned teachers say that any audiovisual, even a simple handmade poster, is effective because, "people don't expect a Hollywood production."

Oh, yes they do! Don't forget that all of us are constantly being bombarded by all kinds of media messages, be it print, video or audio. In order to get our attention for their particular message or programs, producers use the best techniques and state-of-the-art technology to assemble their message. Anything less than a well-produced graphic, tape or film only trivializes the intended message. Judging from any poorly executed vehicle, viewers and hearers automatically dismiss the message as unimportant.

If it is decided to use an audiovisual demonstration (a song, a short film, slides), keep several things in mind. Make sure everyone in the church can adequately hear the song or see the visuals. Spend as much time as necessary to guarantee that all the equipment needed, such as projectors and cassette recorders, are in good working order and ready to go. Waiting for a machine to warm up or for the operator to find the place where the music starts is deadly.

And media should be neither overdone nor overused. The homily is a time for sharing, not for overwhelming the congregation with *Star Wars*-like effects. It is a part of the eucharistic celebration. The use of a film or tape should not make the rest of the Mass anticlimactic.

The introduction in a homily is more than just an attention getter. It is the story of faith offered to the hearers. It is that image, that experience, that touch of everyday, through which listeners can see for themselves the wonders of God. A good introductory device works like the fishing nets, mustard seeds and wicked stewards of Jesus' parables. The most profound mysteries of faith can become real in our own lives.

As much care should be put into the *ending* or conclusion of the homily as was put into the introduction. A good ending ties everything together without being a summary or a conclusion (as in: "In conclusion, I would just like to add . . . ." or "To summarize . . . ." or the dreaded "And so, my dear people . . . .").

The best ending for a homily refers to the introduction—the story, for example, from the Ash Wednesday homily cited a moment ago on the homilist's experience of learning to play the piano:

"I remember how hard it was to learn to make those pauses—to stop and feel the music as well as to hit the keys that made the music. During this Lent, may we work as hard to pause in our busy lives, to stop and feel the Lord's presence in our lives and to hear what he is saying to us during these holiest of days."

At this point in the writing process, the homilist has a working outline—an introduction, main points and a conclusion. Now the homilist is ready to write a complete text.

Keep the words simple and natural. Remember that the people will hear this homily —not read it. If they miss something, they can't go back to read a paragraph again or run to the dictionary. *Roget's Thesaurus* is the perfect tool for finding the most precise word—not the most impressive one.

Use words and phrases with which you are comfortable. If you would not use that word or phrase yourself in everyday conversation, don't use it in a homily. Be grammatically correct, however—which does not mean sounding stuffy or stiff.

And remember that this homily should be communication; it should be sharing. In the eucharistic prayer, the celebrant prays on behalf of *"we* your people and your ministers" and (*we*) "your pilgrim church." So keep that same sense of community in your homily. Refer to *we* and *us* as in *"we* are all in this together." Avoid references to the congregation as *you*—especially, a reference to *you people* which can be perceived as judgmental or accusatory.

After the text is written, read it out loud. For example, does it sound like you? Are the words and images yours, said in a way you would say them to someone with whom you're having coffee?

Now comes the key question: *Does this homily do what you want it to do?* Consider everything that was determined in the thought process (chapter one). In light of the audience analysis done before a word was written, will this homily work?

If it won't, you know what you have to do.

If you determine that the text will, in fact, work, you are halfway there.

Now that you have the homily ready, you must get the homilist ready.

A Homily

Homily for the Solemnity of All Saints

Reading 1, Rv 7:2-4,9-14: I saw an immense
    crowd, beyond hope of counting, of people
    of every nation, race, tribe and language.
Responsorial, Ps 24: Lord, this is the people
    that longs to see your face.
Reading 2, 1 Jn 3:1-3: We shall see God as he
    really is.
Gospel, Mt 5:1-12: Rejoice and be glad for your
    reward will be great in heaven.

(1)   Usually, when we think of saints, we
    think of people of heroic, almost superhuman
    proportions. We think of miracles and acts of
    self-sacrificing charity. We place statues of
    saints with halos around their heads in shrines.

(2)   We also, almost always, think of saints in
    the *past*. But as I listened to the gospel
    reading, the "job description" of being a saint,
    it occurred to me how many real *saints* I have
    met in my first four months in the parish. I
    know people—and you probably know them,
    too—who live lives of sanctity. They don't
    have halos and they are not called saints. They
    don't attract any attention. They perform
    many good works of service that we would
    consider too ordinary to be "heroic."

60

(3)   But they are among the "Blessed" of today's gospel:

(4)   ". . . Blest are the poor in spirit: the reign of God is theirs." Blest are the parents who could have had all the luxuries and opportunities that life has to offer, but who sacrifice so much for their children. Blest is the lady with so little but who gives nevertheless to the poor and doesn't want to be mentioned.

(5)   "Blest too are the sorrowing; they shall be consoled." Blest is the wife who cares for her terminally ill husband, caring for him and loving him. Blest is the husband who faithfully goes to the nursing home every day to be with his wife, who is in a coma.

(6)   "Blest are the lowly; they shall inherit the land." Blest is the cleaning woman who scrubs floors for minimum wage and is embarrassed to come to church because she doesn't have a good dress to wear. Blest is the child who understands and loves his parents, even though his clothes aren't as nice as his friends' and his room is not stuffed with the toys other children have.

(7)   "Blest are they who hunger and thirst for holiness; they shall have their fill." Blest are those people I have surprised in church, praying to God in a moment of quiet in their lives. Blest is the father and mother who spend time teaching their children what prayer is and how

to pray. Blest is the elderly woman whose arthritic fingers can barely move along the beads of her rosary.

(8)   "Blest are they who show mercy; mercy shall be theirs." Blest is that man who is watching his wife die of cancer and who cares for her with love and honor. Blest is the older sister who tries to explain to her younger brother that alcoholism is a disease, so he won't think less of his father.

(9)   "Blest are the single-hearted for they shall see God." Blest is the mother who sacrifices the years she should be enjoying in retirement to care for her crippled son, and who worries what will happen to him when she is gone.

(10)   "Blest too the peacemakers; they shall be called children of God." Blest is that one person I know who is so kind, so gentle . . . who with a few words brings peace to all of us with a smile.

(11)   "Blest are those persecuted for holiness' sake; the reign of God is theirs." Blest is the middle-age woman who knows of her husband's cheating, but who goes on loving him and praying for him and trying to forgive him. Blest is the girl who wanted to be a nun, but whose cerebral palsy rules out the life of a religious. Blest is the elderly priest, confused

by the changes in the church, who is often the subject of ridicule and scorn, yet continues to try to adapt himself even though psychologists tell us not much can be expected from someone so advanced in years.

(12)   These are just some of the saints I have met in my life. There are so many more who have strengthened my faith, who have convinced me beyond any doubt of the existence of God's grace and of the reality of goodness vanquishing evil.

(13)   I invite you to sit back and think of the saints you have met in your life.

(14)   Today we celebrate those saints—the ordinary, who have been neither canonized nor remembered in the church calendar. Yet their lives and their faith are as heroic as any of the great saints. In their simple loving, they point to God just as well as the most beautiful cathedral.

(15)   Through their example, may we live lives of sainthood in our homes and offices and schools and factories . . . that one day, All Saints' Day becomes *our* feast, too.

Comments

Many scripture readings are so beautiful that they are read often — so often that they make less of an impact on us, despite their meaning. The use of St. Paul's lesson on love ("Love is kind . . .") in 1 Corinthians is a case in point. The Beatitudes have become, for many of us, an eight-line cliche, another formula to memorize, along with the Our Father and the Hail Mary.

This homilist has taken the gospel reading on the Beatitudes for the feast of All Saints and has made it a genuine part of the audience's struggle as Christians in the 20th century. In his introduction (paragraphs one and two) he takes the standard image of sainthood from bygone days and redefines it in the present. The homilist shares his realization that saints still do walk among us. Then, he very effectively uses the personal reference/experience device to make his point.

This homily is also an excellent example of good, logical order and sequence. Father works from the concrete to the abstract, from the familiar to the unfamiliar. He begins with the standard image of a saint from past days (the concrete, the familiar), and works from that concept to offer a redefined image of a saint to include saints in their own parish and in their own lives (the abstract, the unfamiliar).

This homily also works because of its *story*. Actually, it is a collection of stories. In sharing stories or examples of people he has met that parallel the "Blessed" of Jesus' sermon, the homilist triggers other stories in the listener's mind. As Father reread the gospel of the Beatitudes to include these new stories of the "meek," "the pure of heart," and "the peacemaker," the individual members of the congregation began to think of people in their own lives as saints. And suddenly, this often heard and somewhat cryptic collection of Beatitudes becomes a meaningful and genuine part of their faith-experience.

Blest are the homilists who speak in stories, for they shall communicate faith.

Chapter 3:

Getting Your Act Together

We've all heard those space-age computers that can speak—technological marvels producing electronic buzzes and crackles that sound like words.

But C3PO from *Star Wars* notwithstanding, a machine's speaking is a poor substitute for the human voice. No machine can duplicate the emotion, tone and many subtle variations in pitch and speaking rate of the human voice. Technicians can program a computer or robot to speak the verbals, but no automation is capable of communicating through the nonverbals—voice emphasis, tone, body gestures—possessed by humans.

If preaching was only a matter of using the right words, many homilists could save time and trouble by printing their texts in the parish bulletin and saying the profession of faith after the gospel. The homilist's delivery makes the difference in communicating the homily. The homilist's voice characteristics and body movements communicate as much as the words spoken: A rise or quickening of the voice, a twinkle in the eye, an arched eyebrow, a nod of the head, or the raising of a hand can communicate attitudes like joy, acceptance, hope, resignation, contempt or urgency far more effectively than words alone.

At this point in the process of preparing a homily, we have produced a well-thought-out text. We have the words—the verbals—that convey the ideas we want to use to communicate the word of God. Now comes what is for many homilists/speakers the hard part: preparing the homilist for the *delivery*. Good delivery means much more than knowing what words to utter. It means knowing how to say those words: the effect of nonverbals on listeners. After looking at the nonverbals of speech communications, we'll discuss a process of rehearsing your delivery.

The voice

Obviously, the homilist's voice has a great deal to do with communicating the homily. The human voice, however, is capable of much more than just producing the sounds of words. Unlike a mechanical voice, every human voice possesses qualities and characteristics that enhance a speech's message.

Intelligibility is indispensable in speech communications. There are two dimensions, though, to intelligibility. *Pronunciation* is the correct way a word is to be spoken. "Nuclear" pronounced "nucular" and "perspiration" pronounced "prespiration" are examples of mispronunciation. *Enunciation* or *articulation* is the clarity with which a speaker actually says those correctly pronounced words. "Guvment" for "government," "gonna" for "going to" and "singin" for "singing" are all examples of poor enunciation.

A common problem for speakers is dropping the sounds of the last consonants of words or syllables. Not only does such mumbling sound sloppy, but it can create problems for the listener who is trying to understand what the speaker is saying. This is a problem especially if the sentence contains a string of words with like or similar-sounding vowels. The only solution is to pronounce those last consonant sounds deliberately, as hard as you can—even if you think you're exaggerating the sounds to the point of sounding foolish. Be assured that it will not sound foolish or exaggerated to your listeners seated in the church or hall. Rather, speaking unintelligibly or sounding like you are speaking unintelligibly, regardless of what you are saying, will make you sound foolish or simple—too foolish or simple for an audience to bother listening to you.

Ralph Waldo Emerson wrote that "nothing great is achieved without enthusiasm." For the homilist, enthusiasm and the *tone* of voice are very much alike.

Remember the last time you were listening to someone whose voice had a certain edge to it? You detected anger or disturbance in the speaker's voice even though the subject being discussed might have had nothing to do with the reason for that edge. That edge is present in all spoken communications. If a speaker is upset, tired, angry or nervous, it will be evident in the tone of the voice. For the celebrant, that same tone is evident not only in the homily, but in the greeting, the proclamation of the gospel, the invitation to pray, and the offering of the eucharistic prayer. Some people do manage to hide negative feelings that might be bothering them, but, for most, our voices, eyes, faces or some other nonverbal will reveal us.

In the same way, positive emotions like joy, excitement and sincerity are also evident in the speaker's tone.

Regardless of the words in the text, listeners will detect the homilist's true feelings and attitudes toward the audience and the subject in the tone of voice. If the homily is merely a chore being performed or if the homilist truly wants to be with the congregation assembled to share God's word and presence, this will be immediately apparent in the tone of the homilist's voice. That's why Emerson's dictum on enthusiasm is important for the preacher.

But Emerson's concept of enthusiasm is not a wide-eyed, golly-gee excitement. A homilist's enthusiasm should be rooted in a love for the ministry and for the people served. It is that kind of caring, sincere enthusiasm that should be evident in the tone or edge in the homilist's voice.

The human voice is able to *emphasize* important words or phrases. Good homilists/public speakers have mastered four properties of the human voice that can be controlled for the purpose of emphasis: pitch, rate, inflection and pausing.

Pitch is the highness and lowness of your voice. The sounds any voice makes correspond to the high and low notes on the musical scale. In everyday conversation, we might use only a few notes, but effective public speakers/homilists will know how to change and vary the pitch of their voice to emphasize words and thoughts. Generally speaking, a higher pitch indicates excitement or urgency, while a lower pitch creates a sense of solemnity or seriousness.

As voices rise in pitch, they tend to carry better than lower-pitched voices. Low-pitched voices become muffled, throaty or breathy, and consequently are more difficult to hear and understand. But voices that become too high-pitched are very grating to the listener (the "screeching chalk on the blackboard effect"). Some speakers with naturally high-pitched voices need to make an effort to consciously lower the pitch of their voices.

Emphasis is also indicated by a homilist's *rate* of speaking. A quickened speaking rate indicates excitement and enthusiasm, while slowing down not only adds emphasis to a vital point, but makes the point easier for the audience to grasp.

Very few homilists and public speakers speak too slowly. Most people speak too fast. A homilist whose delivery seems too slow often has a speaking deficiency; for example, a monotone voice—speaking with little or no variations in tone; or poor phrasing—not combining words into understandable units of thought.

Words are also emphasized through *inflection*—the way a speaker accents or attacks a word. When talking informally with a friend, we all emphasize naturally. But many novice homilists become so stiff when speaking that their voices lose all force and volume. Their vocal patterns become a mechanical monotone of words. The same thing happens to homilists who read their homilies directly from a paper.

Inflection can give meaning and expression to a word or phrase more effectively than added adjectives or adverbs. The following passage, John 10:11, can have a number of different meanings to a listener, just by accenting one word more than another. Read the passage aloud, but each time stress the italicized words:

"*I* am the good shepherd; the good shepherd lays down his life for the sheep." (*Jesus* is the good shepherd, not a pharisee or prophet.)

"I am the *good* shepherd; the *good* shepherd lays down his life for the sheep." (Jesus brings a different set of values to his role as shepherd, not like the values of those in the shepherding business for money.)

"I am the good *shepherd;* the good *shepherd* lays down his life for the sheep." (Jesus does not come as a king or potentate, but as a shepherd.)

"I am the good shepherd; the good shepherd *lays down his life* for the sheep." (Jesus' love for his people is so great he is willing to give everything—including the supreme sacrifice of his own life—for the sake of the "sheep.")

The words are the same, but the change in emphasis through voice inflection results in a different perspective on the passage. Try this same exercise with other scriptural passages. As you write your homily and later as you practice its delivery, be aware of key words that should be highlighted by the natural inflection in your voice.

Sometimes the best thing you can do to emphasize an idea is to just pause and let the word or phrase settle in the mind of your audience.

The piano teacher's advice recalled by that homilist in his Ash Wednesday homily is good advice for homilists as well: Anyone can say the words that make up the homily; the impact often is made in the pause between the words. Stopping after an important idea allows the listener to reflect on your point. In relating a story or before making a key point, pausing can create suspense. A pause immediately after a major point can add emphasis.

In everyday conversation, we pause naturally because we can sense whether or not our words have been understood by the listener. By reading the faces of our listeners, we know instantly whether or not we've connected. We instinctively stop to make sure the idea has been grasped. For the same reason, it is good practice to pause for a moment or two at the end of the homily and let the congregation reflect on what they have just heard. It is like the afterglow effect of theatre lights. For two or three seconds after a spotlight has been turned off, the glow from the light continues to remain visible on the stage. Let your homily bask in its afterglow for a few seconds at its completion.

The body SPEAKS!

In September, 1979, when Polish Cardinal Karol Wojtyla was elected the first non-Italian pope in more than 400 years, television viewers around the world were struck, not by what was said by the new pope, but by what he did. Pilgrims and television commentators alike were moved by Pope John Paul's simple action of extending his arms out toward the crowd and then clasping his arms to his chest, as if to hold the entire world to his heart.

That simple yet profoundly moving gesture illustrates how the body and its gestures are effective nonverbal communicators. Body language is very important in speech communications.

Think about the last person you spoke with today. Think about that person's face, posture and hands as you were conversing. Did they not say as much about what he or she was feeling and thinking as the words spoken? It's natural. When we speak one-on-one with someone and feel comfortable, the body goes on a kind of automatic pilot. Our eyes, face, hands and arms automatically make appropriate gestures and movements to accompany our words.

Homilists should understand that standing stiffly and motionless when addressing the congregation is unnatural. The speaker who stands stiffly and erectly may, without uttering a word, be saying: "This is a very formal occasion"; or "I am scared to death of you"; or "I am vastly superior to all of you."

But the speaker who leans forward a little, physically reaching out to the audience, is saying silently but sincerely: "I'm glad to be here. I'm interested in you. I want to share something with you and I think you should and will accept my ideas."

Animated movement is one thing but twitching, pacing and shaking—or what may be perceived by the audience as nervous agitation is something else. So, when you arrive at the place from where you will speak, plant your feet firmly on the ground, far enough apart so that you will not sway back and forth, but not so far apart that you render yourself immovable.

Body movement can also function to regulate or punctuate communication. A chemistry teacher, for example, may move from one end of the lab table to the other to indicate a change of topic, or completion of a step in the demonstration and movement to the next step. If the homilist is comfortable standing away from the traditional lectern for the homily (and it doesn't bother the parishioners), then the speaker can indicate a change of point or topic by moving a few steps to the right or left. The homilist can also emphasize an important point by moving a step toward the audience.

Remember, however, that posture and body movement can work against a speaker. What the speaker might intend to be enthusiastic animation might be perceived as nervous energy to the audience, effectively making the speaker and everyone in the audience uncomfortable. What the speaker may think is a cool, professional exterior may, in fact, be projected as aloofness and a cold, dispassionate attitude toward the subject and/or the audience.

The key is for all body movements to be relaxed and natural. If you don't use your hands, for example, in everyday conversation, then you will not be able to effectively use them in public speaking. Body movements and gestures can't be forced, but the more homilists become comfortable at the lectern, the more they will develop the confidence to "let go," and allow the body to become a natural part of the communications process.

Two parts of the body are particularly effective in speech communications: the face and the hands.

Psychologists have found that the face accounts for more than half of the emotional impact of a speaker's message. The eyes especially create a bond between the speaker and the hearer. We have come to expect eye contact from every public speaker, whether priest or politician. The speaker making eye-to-eye contact is perceived as sincere, earnest, forthright and self-assured.

The eyes, along with the mouth, the eyebrows and every part of the face, are very effective nonverbal elements of communications, indicating or betraying every feeling and emotion from admiration to contempt. When David Brinkley anchored the *NBC Nightly News,* he was often criticized for commenting on the news. But Brinkley's script read like any other straightforward newscast. The difference was in Brinkley's face as he read it. His comments were not in what he said (the verbal), but in the nonverbals—the lifting of an eyebrow or the slightly bemused half-smile on his face.

What David Brinkley did with a half-smile and a raised eyebrow, Nikita Khrushchev did with his hands. While pounding the lectern with your shoe as Khrushchev did is not recommended, using your hands in meaningful gestures can effectively underscore a point.

Say "This is very important" with your

hands hanging motionless at your sides. Now repeat the words, clenching your fist and shaking it as you say "very." Your gesture probably encouraged you to say that word with more vigor and inflection. But naturalness is the key. The effective homilist will know how to incorporate hand gestures to make stronger and more effective points.

Basically, there are three kinds of gestures. Conventional gestures are the signs and symbols that have specific meanings assigned to them by custom or convention: Speakers use their fingers to indicate numbers or raise a hand to indicate a halt to a situation or set of circumstances.

A second kind of gesture is descriptive. When describing an object, speakers might outline it with their hands, or hold them far apart to indicate a large object. Some verbs can be described with a hand movement: Washing for example, can be demonstrated with a hand wiping an imaginary blackboard. When commenting on size, breadth or panorama, make a sweeping movement of the hand or use the hands to indicate proportions. Such descriptive gestures are so natural that almost any speaker can employ them in moderation. An accompanying gesture also makes a word or idea more memorable in the minds of listeners.

The hands may also be used to describe and

emphasize ideas. A simple raised index finger when declaring "The difference is faith" clearly says this idea is important. A clenched fist conveys strength, determination or anger. Cupped or clasped hands symbolize community or completeness, while intertwined fingers indicate integration or unity. Simply extending a hand toward listeners as if offering to shake hands with them is one of the most effective ways of graciously inviting the audience to become part of a program, movement or project.

Again, gestures work only if they are natural. If gestures are forced, you will look like a machine that is a beat or two out of sync. If your gestures are natural and comfortable, timing will come naturally. Although you should be relaxed, gestures must be done with vigor and decisiveness. Like a weak handshake, indecisive gestures fail to make a positive impression and instead convey fear and indecision.

Once the homilist can talk *with* the people rather than talk *at* them, the rest of the body will naturally follow along and contribute to communicating the word of God. It takes confidence, practice and a conviction that the homilist really loves and cares about these people, that they are, in fact, the homilist's brothers and sisters in Christ.

Rehearsing your "lines"

Winston Churchill, one of the great orators of this century, used to practice his speeches, aloud, in his bedroom. Since his first days in parliament, his family became accustomed to hearing his baritone voice echo through the house. Once, a valet, new to the staff, knocked on Sir Winston's door and asked if he had summoned the servant. Churchill gravely replied: "No, I was just addressing the House of Commons."

It should be clear by now that the homilist's text is just a collection of words. Just as reading the script of a play is a poor substitute for actually seeing and hearing the play performed, it is the homilist's delivery that makes the meaning of these words come alive for the audience. That delivery should be just as planned and as prepared as the words of the text. One part of the task in homily preparation is to be prepared *with* the words; it is just as important to be prepared *for* the words.

In terms of delivery, there are three kinds of speeches. First, there is the *memorized* speech. Although all the words are delivered, a homily given from memory often results in a stilted, inflexible delivery, difficult to adapt to changing audience reactions during the presentation. In delivering a memorized homily, the speaker risks becoming excessively formal or rushing through the speech, cranking out the words with little thought or meaning.

There are also speeches that are *read* directly from the text. The ability to read a speech effectively is an invaluable skill when every word of the speech is subject to public scrutiny and in-depth analysis. Unless you are the president or the archbishop, however, read speeches are deadly from the parish lectern. Homilists who read their sermons inevitably sacrifice the natural freshness and spontaneity necessary for real communication.

There is a middle course between memorized and read speeches: the *extemporaneous* speech. This is not the same as an impromptu, ad-libbed or "off the cuff" speech. The strategy here is not to memorize the homily but to know its basic working structure. Here's an effective method of preparing and rehearsing an extemporaneous homily.

Rather than a text, work with an outline, which is as complete as possible. Write the outline in complete sentences, especially if it is important either for effect or clarity to use a specific word or syntax.

Once you have a complete outline, including

the introductory story, the main points in a systematic sequence, and conclusion, talk the outline through out loud. Do so until you have learned the homily's sequence thoroughly and you can express each idea clearly and fluently.

Now, put the outline aside. Rehearse the homily again, out loud, without referring to the outline. You may find it tough the first time through. You may inadvertently omit some points, you may find yourself groping for words, or you may interchange a couple of points—but don't let that worry you. Keep practicing aloud until all the ideas are expressed in their proper order and the words flow naturally and easily. The more surely you command your material, the more poise and confidence you will have as you stand before the congregation.

Use the notes you have in front of you as a safety net, not as a crutch. Nothing written on your notes should come as a surprise as you preach. The outline you have written should keep you on course. Should you lose your place or go off on a tangent (a common problem even with seasoned veterans), your notes should be written to get you back on track as easily as possible.

As you continue to rehearse your homily out loud, you will discover that the gestures and variations in your voice's pitch and inflection will begin to happen naturally. That's the beauty of working with an outline, instead of a word-for-word text. The danger of taking a complete text with you to the lectern is that you may start reading it. It is painfully obvious when anyone who has been speaking to us in a conversational style suddenly begins to read. The head starts to bob up and down as the speaker looks from the text to the audience and back to the text, the speaking pattern becomes very constant and steady, perhaps a bit faster, and variations in pitch and inflection are lost or become mechanical.

If at all possible, practice your homily in the place where you will speak. Get used to the lectern and be familiar with the church especially if this is your first homily in this particular church or you are new to the parish. As discussed in chapter one, the acoustics of the church or hall can pose major problems for the homilist. In especially large, cavernous churches, projected speech echoes throughout the nave—and there is no way you can prevent it. As you practice in the church, get used to listening to your voice reverberate or bounce off the wall. Wait for the echo of your voice to die down before continuing. If you don't, the only thing people will hear will be a rumble through the church.

Electronic sound systems have been the

downfall of many homilists. Knowing what you have to work with (or what you have to work against) will make things go much smoother.

A major concern with any sound system is the microphone. Get used to where it is located in relationship to your face and how it is anchored (attached to the lectern, to be hung around your neck, etc.). The best approach is to have the microphone eight to 12 inches away from your mouth. Don't speak directly into the head of the microphone, but at an angle. This will help prevent the annoying sound of popping p's and exploding h's.

Getting a handle on nervousness

Many homilists/public speakers experience some form of nervousness before a presentation. That's all right; in fact, nervousness is a positive thing in that it prevents the homilist from over-simplifying the task. Anxiety, if channeled creatively, can give the speaker extra energy for the presentation and can put a certain luster in the voice that might be missing if the speaker were too at ease with the speech at hand.

Why do people get nervous? There are basically two reasons. One is that the speaker is not prepared. If that's the case, then the homilist deserves to suffer. Having endured more than my share of unprepared homilists who droned on and on, I can only hope that their nervousness was excruciating.

The second reason for nervousness is an inferiority complex, or variations on the theme: "Hell, I'm no public speaker." Keep three things in mind as you scale the mount of homiletics:

First, you are not vying for an academy award. You're sharing and communicating, not acting.

Second, you are not Peter appearing before the thousands of Parthians, Medes, Alamites, Egyptians, Greeks and other people in town who heard the apostle's first Pentecost sermon. Mass conversions are not the goal here; be open to a little extra help from above in your delivery. As beautifully expressed by the United States Bishops' Committee on Priestly Life and Ministry in *Fulfilled in Your Hearing*, the role of the homilist is "to help people make the connections between the realities of their lives and the realities of the Gospel. . . . Homilists and preachers can help them see how God in Jesus Christ has entered and identified himself with the realities of pain and happiness." So lower your expectations a little bit.

And third, this is God's word you're sharing, not yours. As a homilist, you have been called to serve the people of God. The people know that and, for the most part, are pulling for you. The last thing they want to hear is a bad homily. Remember that the Spirit of the Lord is upon you, just as it was upon Isaiah and Peter and everyone else who has and continues to transmit God's word.

Notice that when you are nervous, your pulse rate increases rapidly. With the blood surging through your body, your breathing becomes quick and short. You should attempt to breathe deeply, not from the upper ribs, but from the "gut"—that is, from the diaphragm, that large muscle that moves up and down between the abdominal and thoracic cavities.

Try this deep breathing the next time you're feeling somewhat tense over your impending homily. Exhale all the air out of your lungs so that your shoulders shrug. Now inhale, deeply and slowly, then let it out again, slowly. Take a few long breaths and then try and project your voice clearly and loudly. You will find that you have greater voice control and power. You may still be nervous, but you should sense a new energy and dynamism in your voice that will give you the confidence to get out there and communicate.

People today seem to value a style of public speaking that is conversational. It comes from the realization that the speaker/homilist is speaking *with* and not *at* the audience.

This is a good time to tell you about Becky. Becky was a student in a college course I was teaching. She was interested in the subject and worked hard. You could see the enthusiasm and interest in her face. Becky was a little slower at grasping the technical dimensions of the subject than the other students, but she always gave her total attention to the lectures.

So, without mentioning her name or looking directly at her 100 percent of the time, I directed every lecture to Becky. Her enthusiastic note-taking and participation in class gave me the energy and inspiration to continue. By reading her face, I knew whether I was making my point or not, and adjusted the lecture material accordingly. Directing the course intentionally to her made it easier for me to be conversational in my approach to the lectures. The hand gestures and voice inflections came naturally and easily. From the students' reaction and my own satisfaction, it was one of the best teaching experiences I have ever had.

It helps, then, to find a friendly face in the audience and direct the homily to that person. As you gain more experience and confidence in preaching there may soon be a friendly face everywhere you look.

A Homily

Homily for the 26th Sunday in Ordinary Time (B)

Reading 1, Nm 11:25-29: Are you jealous on my account? Who decrees that all men may prophesy?

Responsorial, Ps 19: The precepts of the Lord give joy to the heart.

Reading 2, Jas 5:1-6: Your wealth is rotting.

Gospel, Mk 9:38-43,45,47-48: Anyone who is not for us is against us. If your hand should cause you to sin, cut it off.

(1)   Have you ever wondered why, as the advertising industry says, "There's always room for Jello"?

(2)   Jello—a spineless, quivering mass into which have been thrown any number of artificial additives to make it at least attractive to look at, and not offensive if not pleasant to taste. Jello—the food takes little imagination to make and even less effort to eat. Little wonder why there's always room for it—it's hardly anything at all.

(3)   Have you ever wondered what Christianity is all about? Certainly a far more profound question than that first one, but one which I would dare say receives as little attention. I

wonder if a great many people don't think of their religion as they do of Jello: it's there when I want it, it's not too hard to handle, it doesn't demand too much of me—it's hardly anything at all.

(4)   For those who may still be wondering, ours is not a play church, not a fairy-tale religion, not a conglomeration of artificial additives, not an escape from reality. Salvation, after all, is not a matter of wishful thinking, pious daydreaming, or the spineless self-deception of "doing one's own thing." Christ has called us not to the comfort of a foam mattress but to the cross.

(5)   We can take the message of Jesus and bend it, twist it, water it down to suit us, but every now and then we come across a passage in the gospel like the one we heard today where the stark reality of what he is asking comes across with unmistakable clarity and power:

(6)   Either you are with me or you're against me.

(7)   Either you want to speak of me as Lord or you don't want me.

(8)   The demands are hard—but the stakes are high. To be a follower of Jesus, to be a person who is concerned about salvation requires of each one of us that we are honest with ourselves. How often do we explain away our

negligence in regard to our Christian obliga-
tions? How often do we make excuses for the
wrong we do or the hurt we cause? How often
do we figuratively pull back our hand when
we know we would be better off without it?
How often do we kid ourselves into thinking
that God really can't be concerned about the
fact that we're using other people for our purposes; or that we're so caught up with
ourselves that we fail to see the needs of those
around us; or that we're having such a good
time that we forget there are millions of starv-
ing and homeless people in the world?

(9)   The honesty that is demanded of us, even
to begin to follow Jesus, is the honesty to face
up to who we are, to face up to the fact that
no one of us is without fault, without need for
healing and help.

(10)   Our presence here today won't mean a
whole lot if we're not willing to let the message
of Christ touch every aspect of our lives. His
message is not something that there is just
"room for"—it is something which must be living and active in our lives not just on Sunday,
but in every day and in every hour of our
lives.

(11)   To take the gospel as something less
would be to make of it something which it is

not. As we celebrate this Eucharist, this sacrifice which Jesus left us, let us try to face ourselves honestly . . . to see how we fare in relation to the love he has shown for us.

(12)   Let's not leave the church today without resolving to do something about our relationship with the Lord. Let's not leave without resolving to cut off something which may keep us from him. Our salvation is at stake; our relationship with Jesus is at stake.

(13)   For if we are not for Jesus, then we are against him.

Comments

In this homily, an excellent story is made even more effective by the homilist's delivery.

Everyone can relate to Jello, especially a college community like the one who heard this homily. At least once a day that "quivering mass" is served in the school's cafeteria. From the first day Jello appeared on a dining hall tray, college students have been comforted with the fact that, even if the rest of the meal is a disaster, "there's always room for Jello." So the comparison between our attitude toward Jello and our attitude toward faith is a good one.

But the impact was even greater because of the delivery, especially the first three paragraphs. First, the question is posed: "Have you ever wondered why, as the advertising industry says, 'There's always room for Jello'?" Many people in the congregation chuckled when they heard the question either because they were taken aback with the surprising thoughtfulness Father displayed in presenting the question, or because they didn't expect to hear a homily in the formal liturgy of the college church begin with a reference to something as simple as Jello.

Making good use of phrasing and pausing, Father then presents his comparison rather matter-of-factly: "Jello—(*pause*) a spineless, quivering mass into which have been thrown any number of artificial additives to make it at least attractive to look at and not offensive if not pleasant to taste. (*pause*) Jello—(*pause*) the food takes little imagination to make and even less effort to eat. (*pause*) Little wonder why there's always room for it—(*pause*) it's hardly anything at all." That last phrase was said with an inflection that signaled to the congregation that this obvious conclusion was important to keep in mind.

The second paragraph was said with an inflection that paralleled the delivery of the first paragraph.

"Now have you ever wondered just what Christianity is all about? (*pause*) Certainly a far more profound question than that first one, but one which I would dare say receives as little attention. I wonder if a great many people don't think of their religion as they do of Jello: (*pause*) it's there when I want it, (*pause*) it's not too hard to handle, (*pause*) it doesn't demand too much of me—(*pause*) it's hardly anything at all."

The three phrases that depict the typical attitude toward faith are said with the same matter-of-fact tone as Father's review of the merits of Jello (paragraph one). And then the key closing line, "It's hardly anything at all," is repeated with the same inflection as it was in the first paragraph. The effect on the audience was stinging; so effective that the rest of the homily is almost unnecessary.

If you review the rest of the homily, you'll note other phrases and sentences that can be made more meaningful to listeners by delivery. It is not a matter of acting, emoting, or "hamming it up"; it's saying exactly what you mean, communicating the idea in the same voice you would use if you were expressing that same idea to a friend.

The importance of the homilist's attitude is clear in this particular homily. It would be easy to give this same homily and sound judgmental and condemning (particularly in paragraph four). The celebrant who gave this homily, however, successfully projected the image, "We're all in this together, folks, you and I." Those particular words were never spoken, but the attitude was evident in his voice. When Father referred to "we," he meant it.

The examples used in paragraphs eight and 10 are also effective, because they are simple and real. They're not dramatic, earth-shattering issues; instead, they are attitudes we all operate under at one time or another.

I wonder how many students had Jello at brunch that Sunday morning.